# Iona Community

# Love from ROM
# BELOW

by

## JOHN BELL & GRAHAM MAULE

with

## The Wild Goose Worship Group

## VOLUME 3
### of
## WILD GOOSE SONGS

### The Seasons of Life,
### the Call to Care, and
### the Celebrating Community

D0222704

First Published 1989

Revised 1992

Reprinted 1998

For
all the folk on the ground
who have shown us
love from below

The Wild Goose is a Celtic symbol of the Holy Spirit.
It serves as the Trademark of Wild Goose Publications.

**Wild Goose Publications**

The Publishing Division of The Iona Community
Pearce Institute, 840 Govan Road, GLASGOW G51 3UU
Tel. (0141) 445 4561

Printed in Great Britain by The Cromwell Press, Trowbridge.

# CONTENTS

Page

**6**        **INTRODUCTION TO VOLUME THREE**

**11**       **SEASONS OF LIFE**
             (songs of the stages of daily experience)

**47**       **THE CALL TO CARE**
             (songs of the commitment we share with
             Christ to love and serve the world )

**91**       **THE CELEBRATING COMMUNITY**
             (songs for the sacrament of Holy Communion
             and other high days)

**129**      **INTRODUCTION TO CHANTS AND RESPONSES**

**132**      **CHANTS AND RESPONSES**

**142**      **ALPHABETICAL INDEX OF FIRST LINES**

**144**      **APPENDIX**   Other publications for use in worship
                            from the Iona Community

# I – SEASONS OF LIFE

12  Today I Awake
14  Love From Below
16  Conceiver Of Both Heaven and Earth
18  Bridegroom And Bride
20  Blessing The Marriage
22  God Beyond Glory
24  Lord And Lover Of Creation
26  Stumbling Blocks And Stepping Stones
30  Thirsting For God
32  Hear Me Lord, And Draw Near
34  Gifts That Last
36  When Grief Is Raw
38  Nears The Ending Of The Day
41  Stay With Us Now
42  Come, Holy Ghost

# J – THE CALL TO CARE

48  God It Was
50  Though One With God
52  I Am The Vine
56  Blessed Are You Poor
60  The Beggar
62  The Greatness Of The Small
64  From Heaven's Attendant Host You Came
66  A Touching Place
68  We Cannot Measure How You Heal
70  Sing Praise To God
72  As If You Were Not There
74  We Will Not Take What Is Not Ours
76  Listen, Lord
78  Time
82  We Will Lay Our Burden Down
84  God The Creator
86  Take This Moment

# K – THE CELEBRATING COMMUNITY

92 Jesus Calls Us
94 Come, Host Of Heaven's High Dwelling Place
96 Sing And Be Glad
98 The Ground Of Goodness
100 The Broken Body
102 Come, Lord, Be Our Guest
104 Among Us And Before Us
106 These I Lay Down
108 The Hand Of Heaven
110 Bread Is Blessed And Broken
112 O Taste And See
114 O Look And Learn
116 Jesus Is Risen From The Grave
118 Shout For Joy
120 For All The Saints
122 From Erin's Shores
124 The God Of All Eternity
126 Jubilee

# L – CHANTS AND RESPONSES

132 For Yours Is The Kingdom
133 He Became Poor
134 Be Still
135 Miserere Nobis
135 O Brother Jesus
136 Aaronic Blessing
137 NINIAN SETTING
137 Kyrie
138 Sanctus
140 Benedictus
141 Agnus Dei

# AN
# INTRODUCTION
# TO
# "LOVE FROM BELOW"

Volumes One and Two of *Wild Goose Songs* concentrated on the Life of Christ. In this third volume we have included songs which deal more with the life of Christ's disciples. The songs are still firmly rooted in the scriptures but allow for the celebration of our experience of faith, rather than re-telling the events in the gospels.

In SEASONS OF LIFE, we deal both with the celebration of the beginning and ending of each day and with the similar stages in individual lives. In this connection, it may be appropriate to draw attention in advance to the fact that *When Grief Is Raw* can be sung to a number of known hymn tunes. Funerals are not the places to teach new melodies, yet they often suffer for lack of words suited to the occasion.

Similarly, the four wedding hymns are set to well known tunes and experience confirms that however much a tune like *Sussex Carol* may have natural Christmas overtones, these are quickly forgotten when used in the marriage setting.

But because life is not all births, deaths and marriages, we have included a few songs of experience, two of them drawn directly from the psalms, which allow us to offer to God the frustrations and uncertainties of life. We should do this without fear. After all, when Jesus ascended to heaven, among those worshipping at his feet were 'some who doubted'.

THE CALL TO CARE reflects the summons of God to ordinary and unusual people throughout the ages and also to us who are asked to live our commitment in imitation of Christ.

We have enjoyed setting the paraphrase of the great hymn of Christ's servanthood in Philippians Ch. 2 to the tune *Jerusalem*, beloved of Last Night of the Proms, which, for obvious national associations, is not always sung gustily in Scotland.

Hymns in this section may be used for confirmations, commissionings, ordinations or any other occasion when the decision of people to follow Jesus is central to the focus of the worship.

Section 3, THE CELEBRATING COMMUNITY, is concerned mostly with songs suitable for the sacrament of Holy Communion. Some of the hymns are preparatory to the sacrament; some may be sung during the sharing of bread and wine; some are evocative of the Communion of Saints gathered, invisibly, round the table; and some are songs of thanksgiving.

An oddity among them is *The Broken Body* set to the beautiful English folk-tune *Barbara Allen*. This song originated in an event where it was not possible, for reasons of tradition, denomination and history, for everyone to share the Lord's Supper. So we offered our pain and our prayers for unity instead, and commend that practice to others.

*From Erin's Shore* and *Jubilee* are unashamedly in-house productions, written to celebrate the Jubilee of the Iona Community, but not localized to that event or organization only.

We are sometimes asked why guitar chords don't appear in our music. The reason is two-fold. In many of our tunes the harmony changes too quickly or uses notes which it would be difficult to produce on a guitar.

But more than that, we are keen that people should learn to sing on their own and in harmony. The Worship Group we lead has 16 members of whom only a minority read music fluently. Yet that does not prevent all of us from singing in parts. For the past century religious music has relied so much on organ or piano or guitar that the beauty and potential of the human voice has been forgotten and the joy of singing in harmony has become, in many places, a long lost experience. We want to encourage people to redeem that loss. It can be done. All it needs is the willingness to learn − something which is as much a prerequisite for worship as it is for cooking or driving a car.

Acquaintances from Africa consistently amaze us at their vocal abilities, especially when we discover that their songs are not written down in staff or sol-fa notation. Then we learn that they use their ears and their intelligence in a way which makes European Christians seem apathetic if not downright lazy.

In this volume, as in the previous two, there lies much unseen work of the Community's office staff, particularly Maggie Simpson, and publication staff, particularly Michael Lee. To them and to all whose enquiries, suggestions, complaints and encouragement have fueled our imagination, we express our heartfelt gratitude.

John L. Bell
Graham A. Maule
March 1989

Please note:   In this revised edition there are guitar chords given with some songs. These do **not** always correspond to harmony settings.

A companion cassette entitled *LOVE FROM BELOW*, recorded by the Wild Goose Worship Group is available with this volume.

# SEASONS OF LIFE

# TODAY I AWAKE

Tune:   SLITHERS OF GOLD (JLB)

brightly
To-day I a-wake _____ and God is be-fore me. _____ At

night, as I dreamt, ___ he sum-moned the day; _____ for

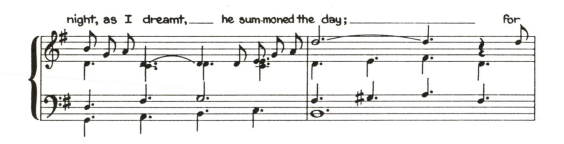

God ne-ver sleeps ___ but pa-tterns the morn — ing with

sli-thers of gold _____ or glo-ry in grey. _____

1. Today I awake
   And God is before me.
   At night, as I dreamt,
   He summoned the day;
   For God never sleeps
   But patterns the morning
   With slithers of gold
   Or glory in grey.

2. Today I arise
   And Christ is beside me.
   He walked through the dark
   To scatter new light.
   Yes, Christ is alive,
   And beckons his people
   To hope and to heal,
   Resist and invite.

3. Today I affirm
   The Spirit within me
   At worship and work,
   In struggle and rest.
   The Spirit inspires
   All life which is changing
   From fearing to faith,
   From broken to blest.

4. Today I enjoy
   The Trinity round me,
   Above and beneath,
   Before and behind;
   The Maker, the Son,
   The Spirit together —
   They called me to life
   And call me their friend.

This is a morning hymn in the Celtic tradition, celebrating the presence of the God-in-three-persons throughout creation and the direct relationship of worship and work. It should be sung brightly and with a steady beat.

# LOVE FROM BELOW

Tune:   A LITTLE CHILD (JLB)

gently but firmly

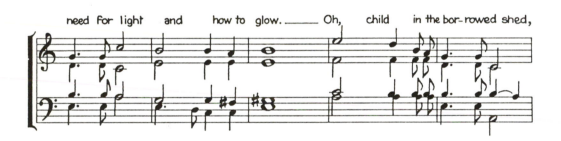

1.  A little child in a bed of night
    Long, long ago,
    Convinced the world of its need for light
    And how to glow.
    Oh, child in the borrowed shed,
    Clearly you show
    How God in splendour reveals for earth
    Love from below.

2.  A little child from her mother's knee
    Squeezed through a space
    To find herself in a tradesman's arms,
    Smile on her face.
    Oh, child saved from adult scorn,
    Central your place
    When Christ embraces you as the key
    To heaven's grace.

3.  A little child in a random crowd
    Tired and unfed,
    Arrived to place in a stranger's hands
    Fishes and bread.
    Oh, child by your selflessness,
    Others you've led
    To share with all what they called their own,
    As Jesus said.

4.  A little child to the font we bring
    Here to entwine
    His/Her life with that of the Lord of Love,
    Jesus, the Vine.
    Oh,  child as you're christened here
    Through word and sign,
    God's finger writes in your heart the words
    "Now you are mine."

Where children are present for the sacrament of baptism, this hymn is particularly appropriate as it underlines the centrality of the child in the life of the Christian community.

Where there are two or more baptisms, the last verse should be altered thus:

    These children now to the font we bring
    Here to entwine
    Their lives with that of the Lord of Love,
    Jesus, the Vine.
    On all who are christened here,
    Through word and sign,
    God's finger writes in their hearts the words
    "Now you are mine."

# CONCEIVER OF
# BOTH HEAVEN AND EARTH

Tune:   CALUM (JLB)

1.  Conceiver of both heaven and earth,
    Our words are feeble to express
    The wonder of the world you bore,
    Creating out of randomness.

2.  Both rich and barren, damp and dry,
    You nurtured and endowed the land,
    Providing with a mother's care,
    Protecting with a father's hand.

3.  And in your image we are made,
    And with imagination blessed;
    Born to bear children and bear fruit
    And in our love find yours expressed.

4.  Be present in the gentle joy
    Surrounding this small babe we bring:
    Baptise her/him with the Spirit's kiss,
    While friends in heaven and angels sing.

5.  Let Christ's own love embrace her/his home
    Where children find their proper place –
    Welcomed and wanted, listened to,
    Signs of the kingdom, gifts of grace.

6.  And bless us who, for this child's sake,
    Will visit, marvel, watch and pray.
    Refine our lives as witnesses
    To heavenly love made real today.

In some churches it is the practice to bring the baptismal party into the sanctuary during a hymn. If that is done with this hymn, the party should enter at verse 3.

Where there are two or more baptisms, the words may easily be changed:

|      |                 |                   |
|------|-----------------|-------------------|
| v4:  | this small babe | – these small babes |
| v4:  | her/him         | – them            |
| v5:  | her/his home    | – their homes     |
| v6:  | this child's    | – children's      |

An alternative tune, suitable for baptism is *O Waly Waly*, found on p. 124

# BRIDEGROOM AND BRIDE

Tune:   SLANE (Irish Trad.)

moderato

God, in the plan-ning and pur-pose of life,_____

hal-lowed the un-ion of hus-band and wife:_____

this we em-bo-dy where love is dis-played,_____

rings are pre-sent-ed and pro-mi-ses made._____

words © 1989 The Iona Community

1. God, in the planning and purpose of life,
   Hallowed the union of husband and wife:
   This we embody where love is displayed,
   Rings are presented and promises made.

2. Jesus was found, at a similar feast,
   Taking the roles of both waiter and priest,
   Turning the worldly towards the divine,
   Tears into laughter and water to wine.

3. Therefore we pray that his spirit preside
   Over the wedding of bridegroom and bride,
   Fulfilling all that they've hoped will come true,
   Lighting with love all they dream of and do.

4. Praise then the Maker, the Spirit, the Son,
   Source of the love through which two are made one.
   God's is the glory, the goodness and grace
   Seen in this marriage and known in this place.

It is preferable to use this hymn at the beginning of a marriage service, before the vows are made. The ancient Irish tune is well known to most people, and harmonised versions can be found in most hymn books.

# BLESSING THE MARRIAGE

Tune:  SUSSEX CAROL (English Trad.)

That hu—man life might ri—cher be, that
child—ren may be named and known, that love finds its own
sanc—tua—ry, that those in love stay not a—lone,
PRAISE, PRAISE THE MAK—ER, SPI—RIT, SON, _____
BLESS—ING THIS MAR—RIAGE NOW BE—GUN.

1.  That human life might richer be,
    That children may be named and known,
    That love finds its own sanctuary,
    That those in love stay not alone,

*Chorus:*  PRAISE, PRAISE THE MAKER, SPIRIT, SON,
    BLESSING THIS MARRIAGE NOW BEGUN.

2.  As two we love are wed this day
    And we stand witness to their vow,
    We call on God, the Trinity,
    To sanctify their pledges now.

3.  Parents and families they leave,
    Their own new family to make;
    And, sharing what their pasts have taught,
    They shape it for the future's sake.

4.  This is as God meant it to be,
    That man and woman should be one
    And live in love and love through life,
    As Christ on earth has taught and done.

5.  Then, bless the bridegroom, bless the bride,
    The dreams they dream, the hopes they share;
    And thank the Lord whose love inspires
    The joy their lips and ours declare.

Wedding hymns sometimes tend to be dreary. This song, best suited before the vows have been made, counteracts that tendency by being set to a lively carol tune.

# GOD BEYOND GLORY

Tune: SCHÖNSTER HERR JESU (Silesian Trad.)

moderato

God be-yond glo-ry, gra-cious and ho-ly,

in whose rare im-age each life is made,____

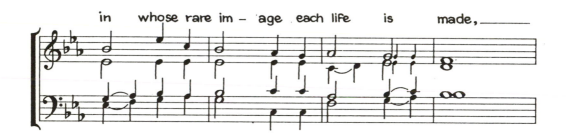

love is the trea-sure, love is the

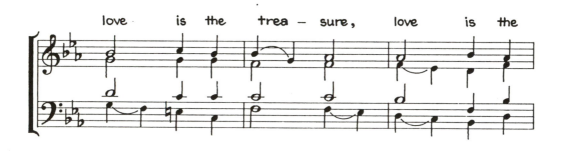

mea-sure of all your Son on earth dis-played.____

words and arrangement © 1989 The Iona Community

1. God beyond glory,
   Gracious and holy,
   In whose rare image each life is made,
   Love is the treasure,
   Love is the measure
   Of all your Son on earth displayed.

2. Binding each other,
   Father to mother,
   Parents to children and friend to friend,
   Love, in its sharing,
   Love, in its caring
   Dares to begin what none dare end.

3. Here, in your presence,
   Love is the essence
   Sealing the vows shared by husband and wife.
   This love confessing,
   Send them your blessing
   To guard and guide their chosen life.

4. When joys are deepest,
   Where paths are steepest,
   Whatever figures in years to come,
   Let love in duty
   And love in beauty
   Embrace their hearts, their hopes, their home.

A song best used just after the marriage has been blessed.

# LORD AND LOVER OF CREATION

Tune:   WESTMINSTER ABBEY (Henry Purcell)

grandioso

Lord and lo — ver of cre - a — tion, bless the mar-riage

wit- nessed now:___ sign of lives no lon - ger sep-erate,

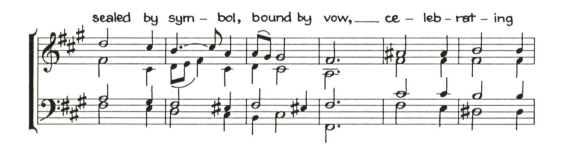

sealed by sym — bol, bound by vow, ___ ce - leb-rat - ing

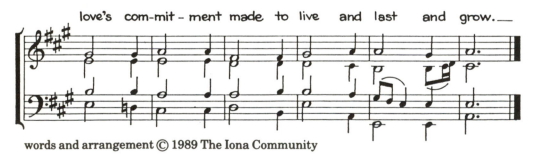

love's com-mit - ment made to live and last and grow.___

1. Lord and lover of creation,
   Bless the marriage witnessed now:
   Sign of lives no longer seperate,
   Sealed by symbol, bound by vow,
   Celebrating love's commitment
   Made to live and last and grow.

2. Praise and gratitude we offer,
   For the past which shaped today:
   Words which stirred and deepened conscience,
   Family life, good company,
   Friends who touched and summoned talent,
   Nourished all words can't convey.

3. On your children wed and welcome
   Here among us, we request
   Health in home and hearts, and humour
   Through which heaven and earth are blessed;
   Open doors and human pleasure,
   Time for touch and trust and rest.

4. Take them hence that, in each other,
   Love fulfilling love shall find
   Much to share and more to treasure,
   Such that none dare break or bind
   Those your name has joined together,
   One in body, heart and mind.

Best sung at the end of a marriage ceremony, the words may be used with other tunes in 8787 87 metre, such as *Tantum Ergo Sacramentum*, if *Westminster Abbey* is not well known.

# STUMBLING BLOCKS
# AND STEPPING STONES

Tune: MARY MORRISON (Scottish Trad.)

tenderly

Un - sure, when what was bright turns dark and life, it seems, has

lost its way, we quest-ion what we once be-lieved and

fear that doubt has come to stay. We sense the worm that

gnaws with-in has with-ered will-power, weak-ened bones, and

words and arrangement © 1989 The Iona Community

1.  Unsure, when what was bright turns dark
    And life, it seems, has lost its way,
    We question what we once believed
    And fear that doubt has come to stay.
    We sense the worm that gnaws within
    Has withered willpower, weakened bones,
    And wonder whether all that's left
    Is stumbling blocks or stepping stones

2.  Where minds and bodies reel with pain
    Which nervous smiles can never mask,
    And hope is forced to face despair
    And all the things it dared not ask;
    Aware of weakness, guilt or shame,
    The will gives out, the spirit groans,
    And clutching at each straw we find
    More stumbling blocks than stepping stones.

3.  Where family life has lost its bliss
    And silences endorse mistrust,
    Or anger boils and tempers flare
    As love comes under threat from lust;
    Where people cannot take the strain
    Of worklessness and endless loans,
    What pattern will the future weave –
    Just stumbling blocks, no stepping stones?

4.  Where hearts that once held love are bare
    And faith, in shreds, compounds the mess;
    Where hymns and prayers no longer speak
    And former friends no longer bless;
    And when the church where some belonged
    No more their loyalty enthrones,
    The plea is made, 'If you are there,
    Turn stumbling blocks to stepping stones!'

5.    Ah God, You, with the Maker's eye,
      Can tell if all that's feared is real,
      And see if life is more than what
      We suffer, dread, despise and feel.
      If some by faith no longer stand
      Nor hear the truth your voice intones,
      Stretch out your hand to help your folk
      From stumbling blocks to stepping stones.

This is the first of five hymns which deal with the pain and disappointment of life. It is not advisable to sing all the verses unless some are taken solo. Verses 4 & 5 may be omitted without ruining the flow of the words.

The tune is not difficult to learn but if an easier alternative is preferred, try *Ye Banks and Braes* on P. 68.

# THIRSTING FOR GOD

Tune:  THIRSTING FOR GOD (JLB)

lamentoso

Just as a lost and thirs-ty deer___ longs for a

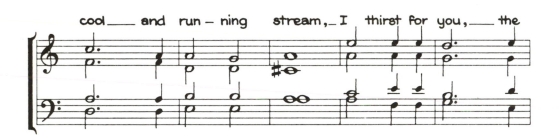

cool___ and run-ning stream,___ I thirst for you,___ the

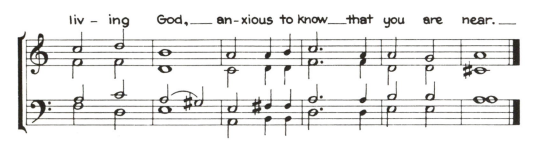

liv-ing God,___ an-xious to know___that you are near.___

1. Just as a lost and thirsty deer
   Longs for a cool and running stream,
   I thirst for you, the living God,
   Anxious to know that you are near.

2. Both day and night I cry aloud;
   Tears have become my only food,
   While all around cruel voices ask,
   'Where is your God? Where is your God?'

3. Broken and hurt, I call to mind
   How in the past I served the Lord,
   Worshipped and walked with happy crowds
   Singing and shouting praise to God.

4. Why am I now so lost and low?
   Why am I troubled and confused?
   Given no answer, still I hope
   And trust my Saviour and my God.

In Psalm 42, the writer expresses feelings of misery and abandonment in amazingly tender and beautiful language. This song paraphrases the psalm and is set to a very simple but evocative tune.

# HEAR ME, LORD, AND DRAW NEAR

Tune: TROUBLED SOUL (JLB)

slowly and steadily

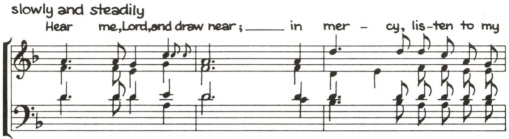

Hear me, Lord, and draw near; in mer - cy, lis-ten to my

plea: I am worn out, wea - ry and ex-

- haust - ed and my soul is troub-led deep with-in me.

words and music © 1989 The Iona Community

1. Héar me, Lórd, and draw néar;
   In mércy, listen to my pléa:
   I am worn oút, wéary and exháusted
   And my sóul is tróubled deep within me.

2. Lórd, how lóng will you tárry?
   Come quíckly, cóme to my distréss;
   In kíndness, réscue me from déath,
   Let me sée the dáy when I can práise you.

3. İ am worn óut with grief:
   Every night confúsion fills my mínd,
   My pillow is sóaked with téars
   And my éyes are dím and sore with wéeping.

4. Lórd, you héar how I crý;
   The sóund of wéeping fills your éars.
   I trúst in yóu for delíverance
   And an énd to áll that now deféats me.

The feelings of disappointment with God and urgent requests for God to act are not common in our prayers and hymns. But they are common in psalms, such as Psalm 6 paraphrased here.

To aid its singing, the pointed words should be sung on the first or third beats of odd numbered bars and the first beats on even numbered bars. Where a congregation is not used to singing prose psalms or canticles, such a song should be first demonstrated by a choir or small vocal group.

# GIFTS THAT LAST

Tune:    ARKLET ROAD (JLB)

moderato
God give us peace that lasts___ not through the fear of might,___ but

through the force of love and love of life and right.___ Where

cost - ly wars and wea-pons lure, show us our Lord a-mong the poor.___

words and music © 1989 The Iona Community

1. God, give us peace that lasts
   Not through the fear of might,
   But through the force of love
   And love of life and right.
   Where costly wars and weapons lure,
   Show us our Lord among the poor.

2. God, give us love that lasts,
   Which makes of strangers, guests;
   Which startles hurt with hope
   And for the weak protests:
   What hate or guiltiness emboss,
   Confront with Jesus and the cross.

3. God, give us hope that lasts
   Through passion, and through pain,
   Through danger, doubt and death
   Till life is raised again.
   When dread and pessimism loom,
   Direct us to the empty tomb.

4. And all these things we ask
   In knowledge of your grace
   Which gave the earth its birth
   And bore a human face;
   And with our prayers we give our word
   To serve and follow Christ our Lord.

Often we pray for such things as peace, hope and love without being clear about what it is we are praying for. In this song the gifts being prayed for are recognised both in the life of the world and in the experience of Jesus.

An alternative well-known tune in 6666 88 metre is *Love Unknown*.

# WHEN GRIEF IS RAW

Tune:    PALMER (JLB)

gently

O Christ, you wept when grief was raw, and felt    for those who mourned a

Friend; ___ come close to where we would not be, and hold    us,

hold    us,    hold    us, hold us, numbed by this life's    end. ___

1. O Christ, you wept when grief was raw,
   And felt for those who mourned their friend;
   Come close to where we would not be
   And hold us, numbed by this life's end.

2. The well-loved voice is silent now
   And we have much we meant to say;
   Collect our lost and wandering words
   And keep them till the endless day.

3. We try to hold what is not here
   And fear for what we do not know;
   Oh, take our hands in yours, Good Lord,
   And free us to let our friend go.

4. In all our loneliness and doubt
   Through what we cannot realise,
   Address us from your empty tomb
   And tell us that life never dies.

A ministerial colleague remarked to us that there are few funeral hymns to easily sung tunes which offer the pain of grief to God as distinct from the joy of resurrection. This song is here set to a tune which would be best sung by a choir, noting that the second and third words of every last line are repeated four times in conjunction with the music. However, for immediate congregational use, the Common Metre tunes *Rockingham* or *Angelus* may be employed.

# NEARS THE ENDING OF THE DAY

Tune:  DAY'S ENDING (JLB)

gently

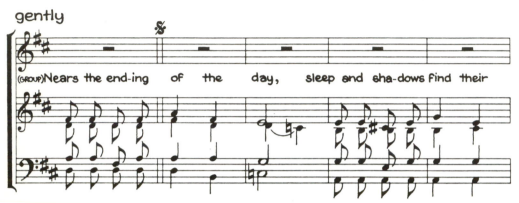

(GROUP) Nears the end-ing of the day, sleep and sha-dows find their

way, (ALL) TURNS THE WORLD BY GOD'S OWN HAND, COMES THE NIGHT TO

(SOLO) Praise the Ma-ker of all time and space, ne-ver

REST THE LAND.

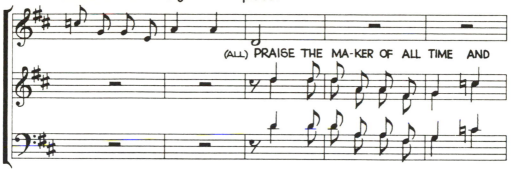

words and music © 1989 The Iona Community

*Chorus:* *Choir:* Nears the ending of the day,
Sleep and shadows find their way,
*All:* TURNS THE WORLD BY GOD'S OWN HAND,
COMES THE NIGHT TO REST THE LAND.

1. *Solo:* Praise the Maker of all time and space,
Never bound to one insight or place.
*All:* PRAISE THE MAKER OF ALL TIME AND SPACE,
NEVER BOUND TO ONE INSIGHT OR PLACE.

*Chorus (as above)*

2. *Solo:* Praise the Maker of all things that move,
Held, yet liberated, by God's love.
*All:* *(Repeat)*

3.  *Solo:*   Praise the Maker of the day that's done,
              Even now preparing light to come.
    *All:*    *(Repeat)*

4.  *Solo:*   Praise the Maker, praise the Maker's Son,
              Praise the Spirit binding all in one.
    *All:*    *(Repeat)*

When singing this vesper, have a small ensemble or choir alternate with the full congregation. In the music copy, the small group sings the words in standard letters, and everyone else repeats what has been sung.

# STAY WITH US NOW

Tune:   DARKNESS (JLB)

*Response:*  JESUS CHRIST, LORD OF ALL,
STAY WITH US NOW.

*Cantor:*  1.  Day is almost ended:

2.  Find your way among us:

3.  Listen to the anxious:

4.  Sit beside the lonely:

5.  Contradict the callous:

6.  Comfort and disturb us:

7.  Do not ever leave us:

8.  Even when we doubt you:

9.  Maker of tomorrow:

10.  Keep us through the darkness:

This very simple vesper consists of a repeated refrain with a solo voice
calling the short phrases in between. Not all the verses need to be used
and they can easily be added to as the occasion demands.

words and music © 1989 The Iona Community

# COME, HOLY GHOST

Tune:  AYE WAUKIN O (Scottish Trad.)

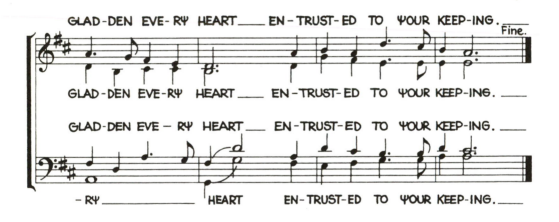

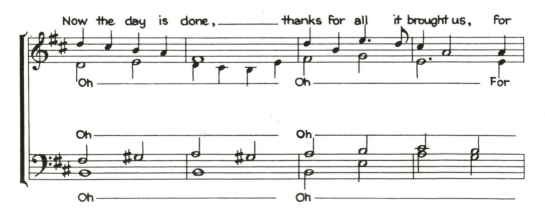

what we met or missed___ and how that touched or taught us.___ D.C.

what we met or missed___ and how that taught us.___

For what we met or missed and how that taught us.___

For what we met or missed and how that taught us.___

*Chorus:* COME, HOLY GHOST,
      SOON WE SHOULD BE SLEEPING.
      GLADDEN EVERY HEART
      ENTRUSTED TO YOUR KEEPING.

1.   Now the day is done,
     Thanks for all it brought us,
     For what we met or missed
     And how that touched or taught us.

2.   Bless the ones we love,
     Bless the ones we weary
     And bless the ones whose lives
     Are empty, done or dreary.

3.   Let our bodies rest,
     Free our minds for dreaming
     And shed the light of Christ
     To set our spirits gleaming.

The tune comes from an old Scottish evening song. For its best use, have a small group sing the verses, and everyone join the chorus. The words underlined thus _____ indicate words sung by alto, tenor and bass voices.

# THE CALL TO CARE

# GOD IT WAS

Tune:   JESUS CALLS US (Gaelic Air adapted)

briskly

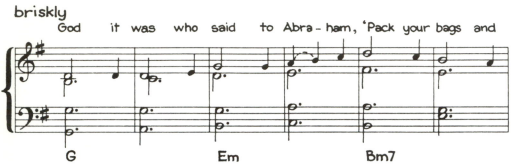

God it was who said to Abra-ham, 'Pack your bags and

G          Em          Bm7

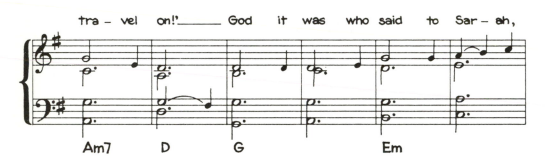

tra-vel on!'____ God it was who said to Sar-ah,

Am7       D       G              Em

'Smile and soon you'll bear a son!'__ Trave-lling folk and ag-ed

Bm7          Am7    D    G    Dm    G

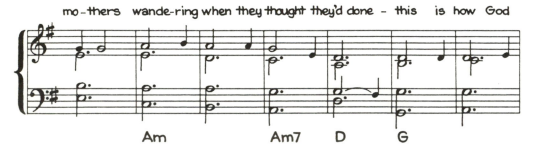

mo-thers wande-ring when they thought they'd done - this is how God

Am          Am7    D    G

calls his peop – le, los – ing all be–cause of One. ____

Em   Bm7   Am7   G

1.  God it was who said to Abraham,
    'Pack your bags and travel on!'
    God it was who said to Sarah,
    'Smile and soon you'll bear a son!'
    Travelling folk and aged mothers
    Wandering when they thought they'd done –
    This is how God calls his people,
    Losing all because of One.

2.  God it was who said to Moses,
    'Save my people, part the sea!'
    God it was who said to Miriam,
    'Sing and dance to show you're free!'
    Shepherd-saints and tambourinists
    Doing what he knew they could –
    This is how God calls his people,
    Liberating what they should.

3.  God it was who said to Joseph,
    'Down your tools and take your wife!'
    God it was who said to Mary,
    'In your womb I'll start my life!'
    Carpenter and country maiden
    Leaving town and trade and skills –
    This is how God calls his people,
    Moving them through what he wills.

4.  Christ it was who said to Matthew,
    'Leave your books and follow me!'
    Christ it was who said to Martha,
    'Listen first, then make the tea!'
    Civil servants and housekeepers,
    Changing places at a cost –
    This is how Christ calls disciples,
    Finding those he knew were lost.

5.  In this crowd of common people,
    Once unknown, whom we revere,
    God calls us to share his purpose
    Starting now and starting here.
    So we celebrate his calling,
    So we prize and praise his choice,
    As we pray that through this company
    God will act and raise his voice.

This song of discipleship, by virtue of the people it celebrates, can never be sung with a straight face. It is best sung with four individuals taking the first four verses and the whole company sharing the last verse. The tune comes from the Isle of Lewis and has been slightly adapted. Its name refers to the hymn to which it was originally set. See P. 92 for a lower setting of the tune.

# THOUGH ONE WITH GOD

Tune:   JERUSALEM (C.H.H.Parry, 1848 – 1918)

with fervour

Though one with God, __ yet not by might __ did Christ his eq-ual sta - tus claim: __ in-stead he gave __ up all he had __ and as a hum-ble ser- vant came. __ In world-ly

form,____ of wom-an born,____ he lived at one ____ with hu-man-

-kind _____ and strode and stum – bled to the

cross____ that we the path to life might find. _____

1.  Though one with God, yet not by might
    Did Christ his equal status claim:
    Instead he gave up all he had
    And as a humble servant came.
    In worldly form, of woman born,
    He lived at one with humankind
    And strode and stumbled to the cross
    That we the path to life might find.

2.  Therefore God raised him after death,
    Raised him to reign in earth and heaven:
    The one whom we considered least,
    The greatest name by God was given.
    And so, to honour Jesus' name,
    All who have life or are to be
    Shall kneel proclaiming 'Christ is Lord!'
    And worship God eternally.

The words are a paraphrase of the great hymn on Christ's life found in the 2nd chapter of the letter to the Philippians. It is here allied to a great tune, not too frequently sung in Scotland because of its direct reference to a piece of very English legend. Most standard British church hymnbooks should contain the full harmonised setting of *Jerusalem*.

# I AM THE VINE

Tune:   VINE AND BRANCHES (JLB)

moderato

I am the Vine and you the bran-ches, pruned and pre-

-pared for all to see;____ cho-sen to bear the

fruit of hea-ven If you re-main and trust in me.____ Fine.

For on your own,____ what can you dare?____ Left to your-

For,____ for on your own, what can you dare? Your-

For on your own,____ what can you dare? Your-

- selves   no   sap   you   share: ____   bran-ches that   serve ____

- selves   no   sap   can   share:   bran - ches, bran-ches that

- selves   no   sap   can   share: ____   bran-ches that

their   own de-sire ____   Find them-selves bro-ken as   fuel   for   Fire. ____

D.C.

serve   their own de-sire   are   bro-ken as   fuel   for   Fire. ____

serve ____ their own de-sire   are   bro-ken as   fuel   for   Fire. ____

1.  I am the Vine and you the branches,
    Pruned and prepared for all to see;
    Chosen to bear the fruit of heaven
    If you remain and trust in me.
        **For** on your own, what can you dare?
        Left to yourself no sap you share:
        **Branches** that serve their own desire
        Find themselves broken as fuel for fire.

2.  Stay close and root my words within you:
    What you request you soon shall have
    Until you carry fruit in plenty,
    Nourished and fertile through my love.
        **In** this is glory given to God
        As you, my chosen ones, prove my word:
        **Gladly** obedient to my commands,
        Love shall fulfil what love demands.

3. So let my joy complete and cheer you
   In whom my hope and kingdom lies;
   Loving each other as I loved you,
   Savour that love which never dies.
   
       **Though** as a servant to you I came,
       <u>You are not</u> summoned <u>to bear that name.</u>
       <u>I call you friends; you are my choice;</u>
       In you I trust <u>and in you rejoice.</u>

4. I am the Vine and you the branches,
   Pruned and prepared for all to see;
   Chosen to bear the fruit of heaven
   If you remain and trust in me.

This is a paraphrase of St. John 15, v.1 – 17. Although it does not have a chorus it is very enjoyable to sing if the first stanza in each verse is sung by everyone and the second stanza sung by a choir or quartet. This kind of relationship between congregation and choir should be encouraged. It has a long pedigree, dating back to Bach and is a welcome change to the 'normal' practice of the choir doing their thing inevitably on their own.

To save writing out the harmony parts in full, those words underlined in the text are the only ones sung in the requisite lines by alto and bass and the words which are boldest type are sung twice, by alto.

# BLESSED ARE YOU POOR

Tune:   ST. LUKE (JLB)

with vigour

Bless-ed, bless-ed are you poor; the king-dom of God is

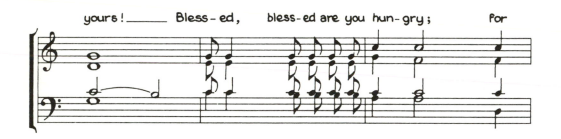

yours! Bless-ed, bless-ed are you hun-gry; for

soon you will be filled! Bless-ed now are you

You

Bless-ed now are you

You

1. Blessed, blessed are you poor;
   The kingdom of God is yours!
   Blessed, blessed are you hungry;
   For soon you will be filled!
   Blessed now are you (YOU) weepers
   Even though your eyes are filled with tears;
   Soon you will be found (FOUND) laughing
   Overcoming sadness, hurt and fears.

2. Blessed, blessed are you all
   When people hate and jeer.
   Bless them, bless the ones who scorn
   Because you trust in me.
   When oppression comes,(THEN) face it;
   Face it with your feet and dance for joy.
   Great is the reward (THAT) heaven
   Keeps for those whom hell cannot employ.

3.  Tremble, tremble now you rich;
    Your life of ease is past!
    Tremble, tremble now you full;
    No longer will you feast!
    Tremble you who laugh (LAUGH) loudly;
    Now's your turn to mourn and weep and fear.
    You who were so well (WELL) treated
    Never realised when God was near.

4.  Love, love your enemies;
    Do good to those who hate.
    Pray, pray for those who harm
    And don't retaliate.
    Turn the other cheek; (AND) offer
    Those who want your coat, your shirt as well.
    Give to those who ask; (AND) always
    Love the Lord of whom your actions tell.

Luke Ch. 6 v. 20–26 provides us with a version not merely of the Beatitudes, the 'blessed's', but of their opposite. The words are drawn directly from Luke's text, continuing in the final verse into Jesus' injunction to love the enemy.

The words in brackets are interjected by bass and alto only.

# THE BEGGAR

Tune: BEGGAR'S MANTLE (JLB)

(Hum)

I sit out-side the rich world's gate; I rake the rich world's dross and

Am Dm Em Am Dm E

(Hum)

mar-vel that my pov-er-ty is what you call my cross.____

Am Dm Em Fmaj7 Dm Em7 A

O WHO HAS EARS TO HEAR MY CRY? AND WHO HAS EYES TO SEE? AND

(Hum)

Am Dm Em Am Dm G

WHO WILL LIFT MY HEAV-Y LOAD? AND WHO WILL SET ME FREE?____

C Dm Em Fmaj7 Dm Em7 A

1. I sit outside the rich world's gate,
   I rake the rich world's dross
   And marvel that my poverty
   Is what you call my cross.

*Chorus:* O WHO HAS EARS TO HEAR MY CRY?
AND WHO HAS EYES TO SEE?
AND WHO WILL LIFT MY HEAVY LOAD?
AND WHO WILL SET ME FREE?

2. My plea is for my starving child
   In want and hunger born:
   Though seed is sown, the earth remains
   Too barren to grow corn.

3. My work and wisdom are employed
   To harvest others' wealth.
   A stranger on my native soil,
   I lose both heart and health.

4. My image is on every face,
   My voice in every land;
   But still I go misunderstood
   By those who 'understand'.

5. I am the beggar called your Lord,
   The squatter called your King;
   I am the Saviour of the world,
   A torn and tattered thing.

6. So, love or leave me as you wish,
   But if you seek my will,
   You'll take my hurt into your heart
   And cease from standing still.

This song can be sung very simply by having one person sing the verses and others sing the chorus in unison. The next stage would be to have the verse sung and hummed in harmony and then, if possible, to have the whole song in four parts.

# THE GREATNESS OF THE SMALL

Tune:   KENDAL (JLB)

briskly

He knew the great — ness

of the small — who spied two pen - nies in the plate, —

and felt the trust young hands re - late and blessed them all: —

he said what mat - tered was not large — when — in —

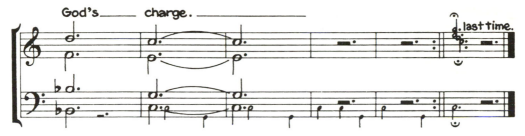

1.  He knew the greatness of the small
    Who spied two pennies in the plate,
    And felt the trust young hands relate
    And blessed them all:
    He said what mattered was not large
    When in God's charge.

2.  He knew the beauty in the small
    Who saw the sparrow in the sky,
    And crushed the corn which seemed to die
    When left to fall:
    He sensed a wonder in each seed
    Which God decreed.

3.  He knew the weakness of the small
    Who dandled babies on his knee,
    And knelt with those who couldn't see
    But dared to call:
    He told the frail they would be strong;
    He stirred their song.

4.  And so the kingdom comes, he said,
    In hidden ferment of the yeast,
    In vagrants summoned to a feast,
    In broken bread:
    What's undervalued in its place
    Is charged with grace.

5.  When we defer to sight or size,
    Believing big is always best
    And falling for the Tempter's test,
    God open our eyes
    To see how Christ, the Lord of all,
    Smiles from the small.

There is no need to accompany this song. If used, the bass notes which provide an introduction should be played softly on piano or organ, giving a rhythmic rather than a melodic thrust.

# FROM HEAVEN'S
# ATTENDANT HOST YOU CAME

Tune: DIAKONIA (JLB)

words and music © 1989 The Iona Community

1. From heaven's attendant host you came
   To meet and mend us on your knees;
   The saviour-servant, still you plead,
   'To know me, love the least of these.'

2. And then to young and old you turn,
   To those who do not know you yet,
   And those whose value none have seen
   Or many see and soon forget.

3. Within the Church, built on your word,
   The call to care finds central place.
   Thus human skill and humble faith
   Are recognised as means of grace.

4. To this vocation now enlist
   Your child whose lips have Christ confessed;
   Inspire her/his heart, direct her/his hands,
   Through her/him may heaven and earth be blessed.

5. And on our shoulders lay your hands
   Confirm the calling none deserve,
   Till all we do and all we are
   Reflect the saviour whom we serve.

The words in brackets are interjected by bass and alto's only.
This song was originally requested for the commissioning of a deaconess or deacon, hence the emphasis on service. It may, however, be used with equal effect at services of confirmation. If sung at an occasion where there will be no possibility of previously rehearsing the tune, other tunes in long metre, such as *Gonfalon Royal* or *Winchester New* may be used.

# A TOUCHING PLACE

Tune:   DREAM ANGUS (Scottish Trad.)

tenderly

Christ's is the world in which we move,___ Christ's are the

folk we're sum-moned to love,___ Christ's is the voice which

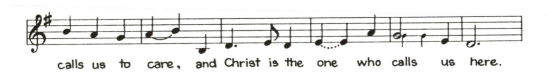

calls us to care, and Christ is the one who calls us here.

TO THE LOST CHRIST SHOWS HIS FACE;___ TO THE UN-LOVED HE

GIVES HIS EM—BRACE;___ TO THOSE WHO CRY IN PAIN OR DIS-

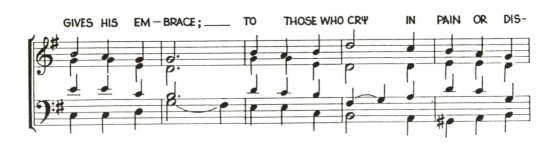

-GRACE, CHRIST MAKES WITH HIS FRIENDS A TOUCH — ING PLACE.___

1.  Christ's is the world in which we move,
    Christ's are the folk we're summoned to love,
    Christ's is the voice which calls us to care,
    And Christ is the one who meets us here.

*Chorus:*   TO THE LOST CHRIST SHOWS HIS FACE;
            TO THE UNLOVED HE GIVES HIS EMBRACE;
            TO THOSE WHO CRY IN PAIN OR DISGRACE,
            CHRIST MAKES, WITH HIS FRIENDS, A TOUCHING PLACE.

2.  Feel for the people we most avoid,
    Strange or bereaved or never employed;
    Feel for the women, and feel for the men
    Who fear that their living is all in vain.

3.  Feel for the parents who've lost their child,
    Feel for the women whom men have defiled,
    Feel for the baby for whom there's no breast,
    And feel for the weary who find no rest.

4.  Feel for the lives by life confused,
    Riddled with doubt, in loving abused;
    Feel for the lonely heart, conscious of sin,
    Which longs to be pure but fears to begin.

This song has been effectively used as written and as an aid to intercessory prayer. In the latter case, one verse may be sung with chorus and in the ensuing silence people may offer names of those whom the words bring to mind.

# WE CANNOT MEASURE
# HOW YOU HEAL

Tune: YE BANKS AND BRAES (Scottish Trad.)

gently

We can-not mea-sure how you heal or ans-wer eve—ry

G    Am7    Bm7    Am7    G    C

suff'-rer's prayer, yet we be-lieve your grace res-ponds where faith and

Am7    D    G    Am7    Bm7    Am7    G

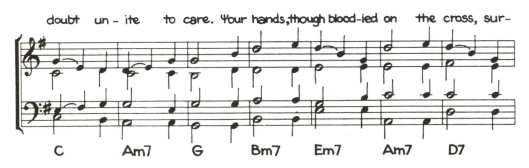

doubt un-ite to care. Your hands, though blood-ied on the cross, sur-

C    Am7    G    Bm7    Em7    Am7    D7

vive to hold and heal and warn, to car—ry all through

G    Bm7    C    D7    G    Dm/F

death to life and cra — dle child — ren yet un – born.

E7      Am      G      C      Am7      G

1. We cannot measure how you heal
   Or answer every sufferer's prayer,
   Yet we believe your grace responds
   Where faith and doubt unite to care.
   Your hands, though bloodied on the cross,
   Survive to hold and heal and warn,
   To carry all through death to life
   And cradle children yet unborn.

2. The pain that will not go away,
   The guilt that clings from things long past,
   The fear of what the future holds,
   Are present as if meant to last.
   But present too is love which tends
   The hurt we never hoped to find,
   The private agonies inside,
   The memories that haunt the mind.

3. So some have come who need your help
   And some have come to make amends,
   As hands which shaped and saved the world
   Are present in the touch of friends.
   Lord, let your Spirit meet us here
   To mend the body, mind and soul,
   To disentangle peace from pain
   And make your broken people whole.

Written with healing services in mind, this song best precedes either intercessions or the act of laying on hands. In our experience, when people are enabled to move during music or song, it makes what might otherwise be an awkward journey much more natural.

# SING PRAISE TO GOD

Tune:  THE VICAR OF BRAY (English Trad.)

**brightly**

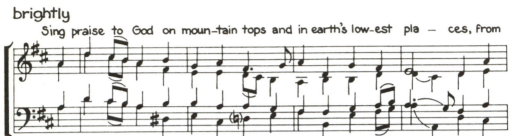

Sing praise to God on moun-tain tops and in earth's low-est pla — ces, from

blue la-goon to po-lar waste, from o-cean to o — as — is. No

ran-dom rock pro-duced this world but God's own will and won — der. Thus

hills re-joice and va-lleys sing and clouds con-cur with thun — der.

words and arrangement © 1989 The Iona Community

1. Sing praise to God on mountain tops
   And in earth's lowest places,
   From blue lagoon to polar waste
   From ocean to oasis.
   No random rock produced this world
   But God's own will and wonder.
   Thus hills rejoice and valleys sing
   And clouds concur with thunder.

2. Sing praise to God where grasses grow
   And flowers display their beauty,
   Where Nature weaves her myriad web
   Through love as much as duty.
   The seasons in their cycle speak
   Of earth's complete provision.
   Let nothing mock inherent good
   Nor treat it with derision.

3. Sing praise to God where fishes swim
   And birds fly in formation,
   Where animals of every kind
   Diversify creation.
   All life that finds its home on earth
   Is meant to be respected.
   Let nothing threaten, for base ends,
   What God through grace perfected.

4. Sing praise to God where humankind
   Its majesty embraces,
   Where different races, creeds and tongues
   Distinguish different faces.
   God's image in each child of earth
   Shall never pale or perish.
   So treat with love each human soul
   And thus God's goodness cherish.

There are few hymns in common usage which offer to God our concern about the environment, despite the fact that for many it is one of the primary issues facing humanity. Here, the stages of creation as mentioned in the first chapter of Genesis, are mirrored.

# AS IF YOU WERE NOT THERE

Tune: ILICH (JLB)

solemnly

As if you were not there,_____ the skies ig-nite and

thun-der, riv—ers tear their banks as-un-der, thieves and Nat-ure storm and

plun-der: all be-ware,_____ as if you were not there._____

words and music © 1989 The Iona Community

1. As if you were not there,
   The skies ignite and thunder,
   Rivers tear their banks asunder,
   Thieves and nature storm and plunder:
   All beware,
   As if you were not there.

2. As if you were not there,
   Famine and flood together
   Usher death, disease and terror;
   Stricken mothers wonder whether
   God heeds prayer,
   As if you were not there.

3. As if you were not there,
   We televise the dying,
   Watch the helpless victims crying,
   Salve our consciences by sighing
   'Life's unfair!'
   As if you were not there.

4. As if you were not there,
   Your Son, when faith defied him,
   Faced a crowd which crucified him,
   Leaving friends who had denied him
   In despair,
   As if your were not there.

5. Because he rose again
   And showed God's love is vaster
   Than the ultimate disaster,
   We entreat you now to master
   Strife and pain,
   Because he rose again.

Throughout the Old Testament, psalmists and prophets offered to God their despair not just about their personal life, but about the welfare of their nation. This song reflects that kind of biblical anxiety which Christians see not resolved but contexted in the death of Christ. To those familiar with Tchaikovsky's music, the title of the tune will be no surprise.

# WE WILL NOT TAKE
# WHAT IS NOT OURS

Tune:   8TH COMMANDMENT (JLB)

animatedly

We will not take   what is not ours:  the free dom of   a   seper ate  place,the future of

a different race,   the un-res-trict-ive-ness  of  space.We will not take what is   not

ours!

D.C.   last time

words and music © 1989 The Iona Community

1.  We will not take what is not ours:
    The freedom of a separate place,
    The future of a different race,
    The unrestrictiveness of space.
    WE WILL NOT TAKE WHAT IS NOT OURS!

2.  We will not take what is not ours:
    The need to fulfil love's demand,
    The right to contradict the smooth,
    The claim of youth to understand.
    WE WILL NOT TAKE WHAT IS NOT OURS!

3.  We will not take what is not ours
    Nor ravage, exploit or pollute
    Till nature mourns her barren state
    And justice limps both blind and mute.
    WE WILL NOT TAKE WHAT IS NOT OURS!

4.  We will not take what is not ours
    And offer then to heaven the dross
    Of poverty caused by our greed
    To win despite our neighbour's loss.
    WE WILL NOT TAKE WHAT IS NOT OURS!

5.  We will not take what is not ours
    Nor dare to enslave or disown
    That loyalty of heart and mind
    Which is a gift for God alone.
    WE WILL NOT TAKE WHAT IS NOT OURS!

The eighth commandment — You shall not steal — is frequently understood as referring to petty crime. The Old Testament gives eloquent witness to its implications far beyond the domestic purse. The plunder of nature and the theft of another person's future is equally condemnable.

# LISTEN, LORD

Tune:   LISTEN LORD (JLB)

gently

LIS—TEN, LORD, LIS—TEN, LORD, NOT TO OUR WORDS BUT TO OUR PRAYER.

YOU A—LONE, YOU A—LONE, UN—DER—STAND AND CARE.___ Fine.

Where the voice that once was wel-come sounds no more,___

send your love to homes turned si-lent hearts turned sore.___ D.C.

*Chorus:*  LISTEN, LORD: LISTEN, LORD,
NOT TO OUR WORDS BUT TO OUR PRAYER.
YOU ALONE, YOU ALONE,
UNDERSTAND AND CARE.

1. Where the voice that once was welcome sounds no more,
Send your love to homes turned silent, hearts turned sore.

2. Where the faith that once was firm is bruised and torn,
Place a manger where heaven's stranger may be born.

3. Where the wisdom meant to heal is spent to harm
Rouse the smothered conscience, sounding heaven's alarm.

4. Where the withered hands and hopes stretch out in vain,
Burst the storehouse of your grace and of our grain.

5. Turn the world and spurn the spite of human greed,
Train our adult eyes on where a child may lead.

This song is essentially a prayer of intercession. The verses should be sung by a small group or choir and, if possible, illustrated for meditation with symbols, posters or slides.

# TIME

Tune:  TIME (JLB)

tenderly

Time,  if on-ly I had

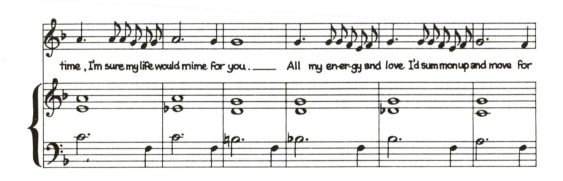

time, I'm sure my life would mime for you. \_\_\_ All  my en-er-gy and love I'd sum mon up and move  for

you. \_\_\_ As  your word would let me know, I'd stop to pon-der,  list-en and to grow    for

1. Time, if only I had time,
   I'm sure my life would mime for you.
   All my energy and love
   I'd summon up and move for you.
   As your word would let me know,
   I'd stop to listen,
   Ponder and to grow
   For you, my Lord.

2. Time, if only I had time,
   I'm sure my life would rhyme for you.
   Every whisper of your voice
   Would make my life rejoice for you.
   As your will would fill my mind,
   All smaller thoughts
   Would soon be left behind
   For you, my Lord.

3. 'Time, oh yes, you have time,
   For all the time is mine,' says God,
   'As is rhythm, as is dance
   And all that hearts and hands applaud.
   You are absolutely free
   To end delay,
   To give your Yes to me
   My child, my child.'

4. Yes, oh help me to say Yes
   With all that I possess, my Lord:
   With my dreams and with my praise
   And all my secret ways, my Lord.
   Let your life and mine be one
   And my obedience
   Offered up to none
   But you, my Lord, my Lord.

This is one of our earliest songs and reflects the kind of hesitation which can be an incentive to faith rather than its enemy.

# WE WILL LAY
# OUR BURDEN DOWN

Tune: LAYING DOWN (JLB)

gently but with a lively rhythm

words and music © 1989 The Iona Community

1. We will lay our burden down,
   We will lay our burden down,
   We will lay our burden down,
   In the hands of the risen Lord.

2. We will light the flame of love . . . .
   As the hands of the risen Lord.

3. We will show both hurt and hope . . . .
   Like the hands of the risen Lord.

4. We will walk the path of peace . . . .
   Hand in hand with the risen Lord.

Ideally, this song should be sung by the majority of the congregation singing the tune and a choir or vocal group singing the harmony. If that is possible, begin with the group singing their part fairly slowly, then add a solo voice singing verse 1 and let the congregation join, a section of them at a time, from verse 2.

It can, however, be effectively sung in unison throughout.

# GOD THE CREATOR

Tune:  BUNESSAN (Gaelic Trad.)

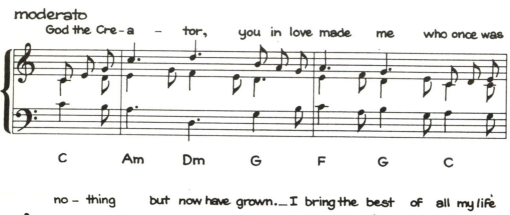

moderato

God the Cre-a - tor, you in love made me who once was

C    Am    Dm    G    F    G    C

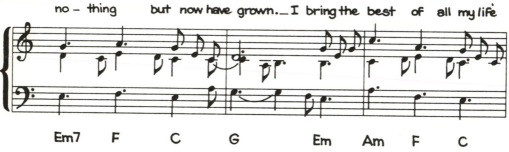

no - thing but now have grown.—I bring the best of all my life

Em7    F    C    G    Em    Am    F    C

of - fers; for you I share what - ev-er I own._____

F    D    C    Em7    F    G7    C

words and arrangement © 1989 The Iona Community

1.  God the Creator,
    You in love made me
    Who once was nothing
    But now have grown.
    I bring the best
    Of all my life offers;
    For you I share
    Whatever I own.

2.  O Christ the Saviour,
    You in love called me
    Who once was no-one
    Lost and alone.
    I pledge to go
    Wherever you summon,
    Making your will
    And purpose my own.

3.  O God the Spirit,
    You in love move me
    Who once was nowhere
    And felt unknown.
    I know my need of
    You for companion:
    All things can change
    When not on my own.

4.  And with the people
    Summoned together
    To be the Church
    In which faith is sown.
    I make my promise
    To live for Jesus
    And let the world know
    All are God's own.

This simple song of commitment can easily be sung unaccompanied.
Most people know the melody well. If felt appropriate, the singular
'me' can be changed to 'us', with further amendments to suit.

# TAKE THIS MOMENT

Tune:   TAKE THIS MOMENT (JLB)

gently and purposefully

Take this mo——ment, sign and space;

D    D/F#    Em7    A

take my friends a——round; ____

D    D/F#    F

here a——mong us make the place

G    D/F#    Em7    C

words and music © 1989 The Iona Community

1. Take this moment, sign and space;
   Take my friends around;
   Here among us make the place
   Where your love is found.

2. Take the time to call my name,
   Take the time to mend
   Who I am and what I've been,
   All I've failed to tend.

3. Take the tiredness of my days,
   Take my past regret,
   Letting your forgiveness touch
   All I can't forget.

4. Take the little child in me,
   Scared of growing old;
   Help him/her here to find his/her worth
   Made in Christ's own mould.

5. Take my talents, take my skills,
   Take what's yet to be;
   Let my life be yours, and yet,
   Let it still be me.

It is seldom that women are allowed to feel that their gender is essentially in the image of God. In verse four of this song, the imbalance is restored. The song may be used at times of commitment and re-commitment and also in the celebration of Holy Communion or marriage.

# THE CELEBRATING COMMUNITY

# JESUS CALLS US

Tune:   JESUS CALLS US (Gaelic Air adapted)

briskly

who,  a – mong  us,  to  our  hopes  and  fears  at  tends.___

F/A   Gm/Bb   Am7   Dm   Gm7   F

1. Jesus calls us here to meet him
   As through word and song and prayer
   We affirm God's promised presence
   Where his people live and care.
   Praise the God who keeps his promise;
   Praise the Son who calls us friends;
   Praise the Spirit who, among us,
   To our hopes and fears attends.

2. Jesus calls us to confess him
   Word of Life and Lord of All,
   Sharer of our flesh and frailness
   Saving all who fail or fall.
   Tell his holy human story;
   Tell his tales that all may hear;
   Tell the world that Christ in glory
   Came to earth to meet us here.

3. Jesus calls us to each other:
   Found in him are no divides.
   Race and class and sex and language –
   Such are barriers he derides.
   Join the hand of friend and stranger;
   Join the hands of age and youth;
   Join the faithful and the doubter
   In their common search for truth.

4. Jesus calls us to his table
   Rooted firm in time and space,
   Where the church in earth and heaven
   Finds a common meeting place.
   Share the bread and wine, his body;
   Share the love of which we sing;
   Share the feast for saints and sinners
   Hosted by our Lord and King.

Though the last verse points towards the sacrament of Holy Communion, the first three stand on their own as a gathering song for any service of worship where the inclusive nature of the Christian community is celebrated. A higher version of the tune may be found on P. 48.

# COME, HOST OF
# HEAVEN'S HIGH DWELLING PLACE

Tune:   ST. COLUMBA (Irish Trad.)

moderato

Come, Host   of heaven's   high dwell — ing   place,   come earth's   dis - pu — ted   guest: find where   we meet   a wel — come home,   stay   here   and take   your   rest.

1. Come, Host of Heaven's high dwelling place,
   Come, earth's disputed guest;
   Find where we meet a welcome home,
   Stay here and take your rest.

2. Surround these walls with faith and love
   That through the nights and days,
   When human tongues from speaking cease,
   These stones may echo praise.

3. Bless and inspire those gathered here
   With patience, hope and peace,
   And all the joys that know the depth
   In which all sorrows cease.

4. Here may the loser find his worth,
   The stranger find a friend;
   Here may the hopeless find their faith
   And aimless find an end.

5. Build, from the human fabric,signs
   Of how your kingdom thrives,
   Of how the Holy Spirit changes life
   By changing lives.

6. So, to the Lord whose care enfolds
   The world held in his hands,
   Be glory, honour, power and praise
   For which this company stands.

These words may be used at the beginning of an act of worship or of a conference. In a more intimate setting, they have been used at the blessing of a house or place of worship. There is a harmonised setting of the tune on P. 122 if required.

# SING AND BE GLAD

Tune:   CAMPSIE (JLB)

**brightly**

Sing and be glad! for this is God's house;

Christ is the cor — ner — stone: wor-ship and

praise which the Spi — rit in — spires we

of — fer to God a — lone.

words and music © 1989 The Iona Community

1. Sing and be glad! for this is God's house;
   Christ is the cornerstone:
   Worship and praise which the Spirit inspires
   We offer to God alone.

2. This sanctuary of fabric and faith
   Grew both from prayer and skill:
   Built on the promise of God, let it stay
   A sign of God's worth and will.

3. Here in our worship, witness and care,
   Here in our work and word,
   May God enable each life to declare
   That Jesus is love and Lord.

4. Here may the lost and lonely be found;
   Here may the sick be healed;
   Here may the doubtful be summoned to serve
   And here may Christ be revealed.

5. All that we are and all that is here,
   All that is yet to be:
   These are the gifts we present to the Lord
   Both now and eternally.

It is not often that new churches are dedicated, but one such happy event in the village of Lennoxtown, near Glasgow, inspired the writing of this song. It may be used at anniversary services as well as dedications.

# THE GROUND OF GOODNESS

Tune:   GOVAN OLD (JLB)

majestically

Praise the Lord, the ground of good – ness, source of si – lence,

sound and time, nour – ish – er of fed and food – less,

cat – al – yst of just – ice, sense and rhyme. _____ -one. _____
except last time.    last time.

words and music © 1989 The Iona Community

1.  Praise the Lord, the ground of goodness,
    Source of silence, sound and time,
    Nourisher of fed and foodless,
    Catalyst of justice, sense and rhyme.

2.  Praise the Lord with city voices
    Pitched in concrete, sweat and steel.
    Let the thousand urban choices
    Always bias to what's right and real.

3.  Praise the Lord as science advances,
    Foundries roar, computers flair.
    Human need, set barriers breaking,
    Fearless, knowing all is in God's care.

4.  Praise the Lord in human pleasure:
    Fond embrace, exciting news,
    Soul-filled thought, creative treasure,
    Talent to inspire, skill to amuse.

5.  Praise the Lord as churches chorus
    Quaker quiet, Salvation brassed,
    Catholic, Orthodox – united –
    Showing oneness meant by God to last.

6.  Praise the Lord, the world's Creator;
    Praise our host and guest, the Son;
    Praise the ever roving Spirit,
    Pulse of life and love for everyone.

Though written for the anniversary of a congregation, the words of this song are applicable to ecumenical occasions or whenever a city church celebrates the environment in which it is set.

# THE BROKEN BODY

Tune:   BARBARA ALLAN (English Trad.)

How can we live as Christ-ians here, untouched by one an — oth-er, lip ser-vice pay — ing
to the name of sis—ter and of bro—ther?

1. How can we live as Christians here,
   Untouched by one another,
   Lip service paying to the name
   Of sister or of brother?

2. Christ is the one who calls us one,
   Who leads us to each other;
   His voice we hear, his Word we read
   And yet his will we smother.

3. One is the water by which sign
   Our lives for God are chosen;
   One is the grace with which our Lord
   From sin ourselves can loosen;

4. But not in bread and wine as yet
   Are hearts and hands united,
   Though each can hear the banquet song
   To which all are invited.

*(Pause)*

5. If our still hands no body take,
   Still bind us in intention:
   Communion must come first through you
   And not by our invention.

6. O Christ of vision and of hope,
   Without whose food we perish,
   Show us the way by which, as one,
   We'll share the One we cherish.

There is a peculiar pain which Christians must feel until the Church is united — that of belonging to a broken body. For reasons of history, tradition, hurt and pride, we are not all able to celebrate the sacrament together.

This song, intended for use at ecumenical occasions, gives the opportunity to offer that pain to God, particularly if there is a pause in the singing between verses 4 & 5, during which time people may pray for Christian unity.

To enable the song to be best sung, a solo voice should sing verse 1 and verse 5.

# COME, LORD, BE OUR GUEST

Tune: DIETWEIN (JLB)

brightly

Come, Lord, be our guest, find your way a — mong us;

you whose word and will sowed the seed which sprung us.

Earth, your for-mer home, _____ still is where we meet you;

there — fore we greet you, _____ Christ our God a-lone.

words and music © 1989 The Iona Community

1. Come, Lord, be our guest,
   Find your way among us;
   You whose word and will
   Sowed the seed which sprung us.
   Earth your former home,
   Still is where we meet you;
   Therefore we greet you,
   Christ, our God alone.

2. Come, Lord, be our guest,
   Join our conversation;
   Free our tongues to speak
   Without reservation.
   Where your people meet,
   You perfect their pleasure;
   Therefore we treasure
   All you have to share.

3A Come, Lord, be our guest.
   Gathered round your table,
   We confess our faith
   More than fact or fable.
   You who made, of old,
   All that earth was needing,
   Blessing and feeding
   Here will make us new.

3B Come, Lord, be our guest.
   Gathered in your presence,
   We confess your love
   Is of life the essence.
   You who made, of old,
   All that earth was needing,
   Blessing and leading
   Show our love your way.

4. Come, Lord, be our host,
   Bread and wine are waiting.
   On your words depend
   All our celebrating.
   Fill us with your love,
   Healing and forgiving;
   Then, in us living,
   Show our love your way.

When this song is being sung at the beginning of a service of worship or a church meeting, verses 1, 2, & 3B should be sung. When it is used in connection with the Sacrament of Holy Communion, 1, 2, 3A & 4 should be employed.

# AMONG US AND BEFORE US

Tune: GATEHOUSE (JLB)

gently

A-mong us and be-fore us, Lord, you stand _____ with arms out-stretch'd and

G Bm Em A7 D G Em

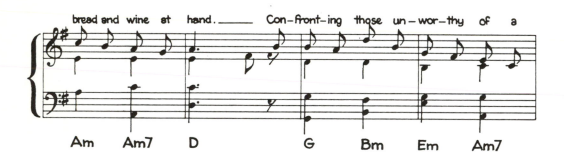

bread and wine at hand. _____ Con-front-ing those un-wor-thy of a

Am Am7 D G Bm Em Am7

crumb, _____ you ask that to your ta-ble we should come. _____

D Bm Em Am7 D7 G

words and music © 1989 The Iona Community

1. Among us and before us, Lord, you stand
   With arms outstretched and bread and wine at hand.
   Confronting those unworthy of a crumb,
   You ask that to your table we should come.

2. Who dare say No, when such is your resolve
   Our worst to witness, suffer and absolve,
   Our best to raise in lives by God forgiven,
   Our souls to fill on earth with food from heaven?

3. Who dare say No, when such is your intent
   To love the selves we famish and resent,
   To cradle our uncertainties and fear,
   To kindle hope as you in faith draw near?

4. Who dare say No, when such is your request
   That each around your table should be guest,
   That here the ancient word should live as new
   'Take, eat and drink − all this is meant for you.'?

5. No more we hesitate and wonder why;
   No more we stand indifferent, scared or shy.
   Your invitation leads us to say Yes,
   To meet you where you nourish, heal and bless.

In some communion liturgies, the Sacrament is preceded by an invitation to come to the Lord's Table. This song is best suited to follow such an invitation. As an alternative tune, Alfred Morton Smith's *Sursum Corda* is most fitting.

# THESE I LAY DOWN

Tune:   LAYING DOWN (JLB)

not too quickly

Be - fore I take the bo - dy of my Lord, _____ be-

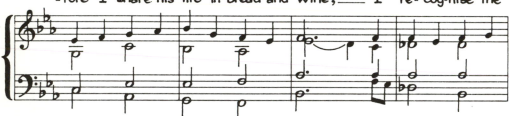

-fore I share his life in bread and wine, _____ I re - cog-nise the

sor - ry things with - in — these I lay down. _____

1. Before I take the body of my Lord,
   Before I share his life in bread and wine,
   I recognise the sorry things within —
   These I lay down.

2. The words of hope I often failed to give,
   The prayers of kindness buried by my pride,
   The signs of care I argued out of sight:
   These I lay down.

3. The narrowness of vision and of mind,
   The need for other folk to serve my will,
   And every word and silence meant to hurt:
   These I lay down.

4. Of those around in whom I meet my Lord,
   I ask their pardon and I grant them mine
   That every contradiction to Christ's peace
   Might be laid down.

5. Lord Jesus Christ, companion at this feast,
   I empty now my heart and stretch my hands,
   And ask to meet you here in bread and wine
   Which you lay down.

As with the previous song, these words are best used immediately before the sacrament.

# THE HAND OF HEAVEN

Tune:   CHARTRES (French Trad.)

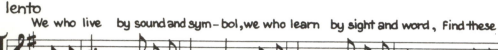

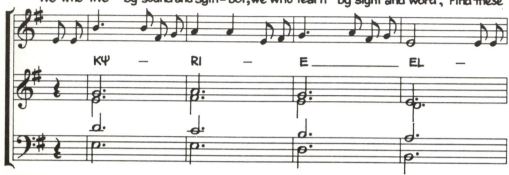

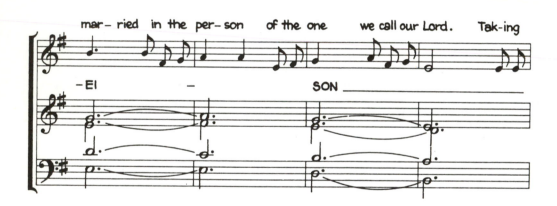

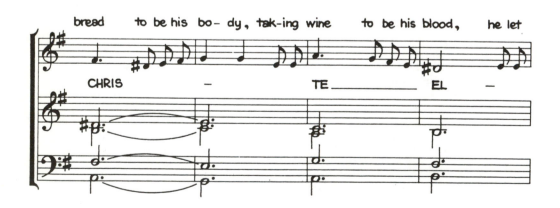

1. We who live by sound and symbol,
   We who learn from sight and word,
   Find these married in the person
   Of the one we call our Lord.
   Taking bread to be his body,
   Taking wine to be his blood,
   He let thought take flesh in action,
   He let faith take root in food.

2. Not just once with special people,
   Not just hidden deep in time,
   But wherever Christ is followed,
   Earthly fare becomes sublime.
   Though to sound this seems a mystery,
   Though to sense it seems absurd,
   Yet in faith, which seems like folly,
   We meet Jesus Christ our Lord.

3. God, our Maker, send your Spirit
   To pervade the bread we break.
   Let it bring the life we long for
   And the love which we forsake.
   Bind us closer to each other,
   Both forgiving and forgiven;
   Give us grace in this and all things
   To discern the hand of heaven.

While it is adequate to sing this song to the carol tune *Chartres*, unaccompanied or in unison, those who wish a harmonised setting might look for the version by David Evans found, among other places, in the Revised Church Hymnary. This choral arrangement, if used, should have the choir singing very quietly beneath the solo voice.

# BREAD IS BLESSED AND BROKEN

Tune: GRACE IN ESSENCE (JLB)

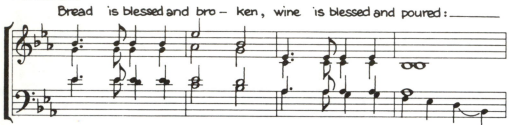

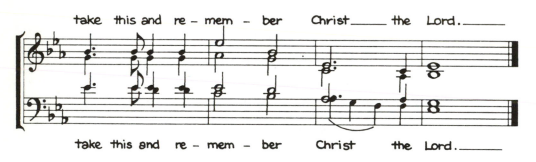

1. Bread is blessed and broken,
   Wine is blessed and poured:
   Take this and remember
   Christ the Lord.

2. Share the food of heaven
   Earth can not afford.
   Here is grace in essence —
   Christ the Lord.

3. Know yourself forgiven,
   Find yourself restored,
   Meet a friend for ever —
   Christ the Lord.

4. God has kept his promise
   Sealed by sign and word:
   Here, for those who want him —
   Christ the Lord.

In many churches of the Anglican and Reformed traditions, the singing of a hymn or anthem frequently accompanies the distribution of the communion elements. These very simple words and tune are appropriate for such an occasion.

# O TASTE AND SEE

Tune: TASTE AND SEE (JLB)

moderato

O taste and see how gra — cious the Lord is!

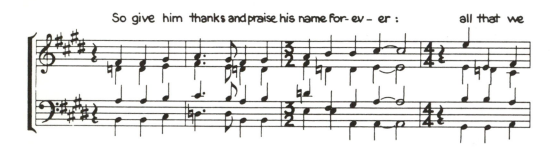

Hap - py are those who put their trust in him.

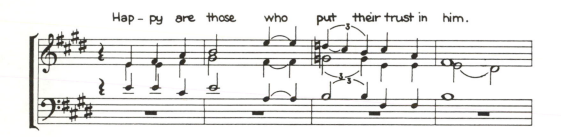

So give him thanks and praise his name for- ev – er : all that we

need comes from his hand._____ -rate. _____
last time.

need _____ comes from his hand._ we ce-leb-rate. _____

need comes from his hand,_ his hand._ rate,ce - leb - rate. _____

1.  O taste and see how gracious the Lord is!
    Happy are those who put their trust in him.
    So give him thanks and praise his name forever:
    All that we need comes from his hand.

2.  As manna fell in the dryness of the desert,
    As water flowed from deep within the stone,
    So God provides for every empty vessel
    True nourishment from heaven's store.

3.  The bread of heaven is in mercy broken;
    The cup is blessed and passed at Christ's command;
    The feast of heaven is shared by earthly people:
    All are made one and called God's own.

4.  Stretch out your hands, touch and taste the goodness;
    Let bread and wine Christ's peace and power relate;
    And let the Spirit stir both hope and healing:
    Such are the gifts we celebrate.

This is more of a choir than a congregational hymn for use during the
distribution of the bread and wine at Holy Communion. The last words
of each verse are underlined indicating that they are repeated by the
tenor and bass voices.

# O LOOK AND LEARN

Tune: SACRAMENT (JLB)

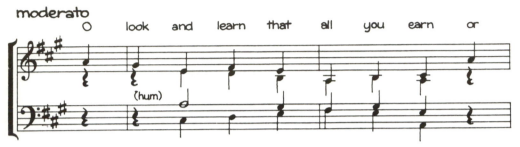

words and music © 1989 The Iona Community

1. O look and learn
   That all you earn
   And own or crave
   Can never save
   The self you dread,
   The world you tread,
   And all I meet
   In wine and bread.

2. O touch and tell
   That none can sell
   Or buy or bind
   Or elsewhere find
   That love of mine
   For foul and fine
   Whose hands reach out
   For bread and wine.

3. O taste and see
   That I am he
   Who thus forgives
   And heals and lives.
   The bread you break,
   The wine you take,
   Is me for you
   And for love's sake.

Another song to be sung during Communion. Either all the sopranos or a soloist should take the tune with the other parts humming quietly beneath.

# JESUS IS RISEN
# FROM THE GRAVE

Tune:   CHILDER (JLB)

Je - sus is ris - en  from  the  grave.

D          Bm          A7          Bm

Je-sus is ris - en  from the grave.  Je-sus is ris - en

D/F#      Bm7      Em7      A      A7/G      D/F#

from  the  grave.  AL - LE - LU - IA!_____

A7          Bm          Em7          A7          D

words and music © 1989 The Iona Community

1. Jesus is risen from the grave,
   Jesus is risen from the grave,
   Jesus is risen from the grave.
   ALLELUIA.

2. Jesus was seen by Mary . . . .

3. Peter will soon be smiling . . . .

4. Thomas will stop his doubting . . . .

5. Jesus will meet his people . . . .

6. Jesus is here in bread and wine . . . .

7. Jesus will live for ever . . . .

Particularly at the Easter season, these words are appropriately sung as Holy Communion is being served. Both words and music are simple enough for children to sing effectively . . . especially in churches where, being precluded from sharing the sacrament, it is good to incorporate them in the worship in other ways.

# SHOUT FOR JOY

Tune: LANSDOWNE (JLB)

*briskly*

Shout for joy! The Lord has let us Feast;

heaven's own fare has fed the last and least;

Christ's own peace____ is shared a-gain on earth;

Christ's own peace____ is shared a-gain, is shared on earth;

God the Spi — rit fills us with new worth.____

1. Shout for joy! The Lord has let us feast;
   Heaven's own fare has fed the last and least;
   Christ's own peace is shared again on earth;
   God the Spirit fills us with new worth.

2. No more doubting, no more senseless dread:
   God's good self has graced our wine and bread;
   All the wonder heaven has kept in store
   Now is ours to keep for evermore.

3. Celebrate with saints who dine on high,
   Witnesses that love can never die.
   'Hallelujah!' – thus their voices ring:
   Nothing less in gratitude we bring.

4. Praise the Maker, praise the Maker's Son,
   Praise the Spirit – three yet ever one;
   Praise the God whose food and friends avow
   Heaven starts here! The kingdom beckons now!

A post Communion song, this requires to be jubilantly sung as if accompanied by a lively brass band. The underlined words are repeated by the bass voices.

# FOR ALL THE SAINTS

Tune: ALL SAINTS (JLB)

words and music © 1989 The Iona Community

1.  For all the saints who've shown your love
    In how they live and where they move,
    In whom they care for, counsel, or visit now and then;
    Accept our gratitude again.

2.  For all the saints who've loved your name,
    Whose faith increased the Saviour's fame,
    Who've sung your songs in chapel or city street or glen;
    Accept our gratitude again.

3.  For all the saints who've named your will,
    And shown the kingdom coming still,
    Who've read the signs and marked them in rhythm, paint or pen;
    Accept our gratitude again.

4.  Bless all whose will or name or love
    Reflects the grace of heaven above.
    Though such as these may never be praised by earthly powers,
    Your life through theirs has hallowed ours.

Saints, as the New Testament teaches us, are not merely stained glass
heroes of the past. They are the people who God has used to spread the
Gospel and their witness, in humble and unpublicised service, is as
acceptable to God as the exploits of those whom we regularly revere.
This song allows us to think of the saints who, in unassuming ways,
have influenced our lives for good.

# FROM ERIN'S SHORES

Tune:   ST. COLUMBA (Irish Trad.)

1. From Erin's shores Columba came
   To preach and teach and heal,
   And found a church which showed the world
   How God on earth was real.

2. In greening grass and reckless wave,
   In cloud and ripening corn,
   The Celtic Christians traced the course
   Of grace through nature borne.

3. In hosting strangers, healing pain,
   In tireless work for peace,
   They served the servant Christ their Lord
   And found their faith increase.

4. In simple prayer and alien land,
   As summoned by the Son,
   They celebrated how God's call
   Made work and worship one.

5. God grant that what Columba sowed
   May harvest yet more seed,
   As we engage both flesh and faith
   To marry word and deed.

Columba is the Irish missionary who landed on Iona in 563 and started a programme of welfare and evangelism which led to the Christianising of Scotland and far beyond. The Celtic Church, of which he was an abbot, was particularly keen to revere God in the life of the world and the processes of human life.

# THE GOD OF ALL ETERNITY

Tune: O WALY WALY (English Trad.)

gently

The God of all eternity, un-bound by

G                        D

space yet al-ways near, is pre-sent where his peo-ple

C          Am7   D            Bm7

meet to ce-le-brate the com-ing year.

Em        Am7   D       D7   G

1. The God of all eternity,
   Unbound by space yet always near,
   Is present where his people meet
   To celebrate the coming year.

2. What shall we offer God today —
   Our dreams of what we cannot see,
   Or, with eyes fastened to the past,
   Our dread of what is yet to be?

3. God does not share our doubts and fears,
   Nor shrinks from the unknown or strange:
   The one who fashioned heaven and earth
   Makes all things new and ushers change.

4. Let faith or fortune rise or fall,
   Let dreams and dread both have their day;
   Those whom God loves walk unafraid
   With Christ their guide and Christ their way.

5. God grant that we, in this new year,
   May show the world the Kingdom's face,
   And let our work and worship thrive
   As signs of hope and means of grace.

New Year is a good time to remember that God is the Lord of tomorrow rather than the patron saint of yesterday.

# JUBILEE

Tune:  JUBILEE (JLB)

with vigour

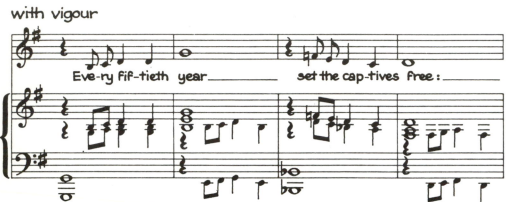

Eve-ry fif-tieth year_____ set the cap-tives free:_____

let a trum-pet blast_____ sum-mon jub-i - lee._____

AND GOD  SAVE  THE PEO-PLE,  THE  POOR, TIRED AND TORN;__ FOR IT'S

Harmony.

IN THEIR LIVES THAT LOVE MUST BE RE — BORN.
(except last time)
D.C.

BORN, RE — BORN.
(last time)

1. Every fiftieth year
   Set the captives free:
   Let the trumpet blast
   Summon jubilee.

*Chorus:*  AND GOD BLESS THE PEOPLE,
THE POOR, TIRED AND TORN;
FOR IT'S IN THEIR LIVES
THAT LOVE MUST BE REBORN.

2. Let the earth find rest
   Where no rest is known:
   Give the world's oppressed
   What should be their own.

3. Cancel every debt,
   Terminate all fraud;
   Let the use of wealth
   Serve the cause of God.

4. Let the hills resound,
   Let the oceans roar,
   Celebrate the good,
   Heaven and earth restore.

*Final Chorus:*    AND GOD BLESS THE PEOPLE,
THE POOR, TIRED AND TORN
FOR IT'S IN THEIR LIVES
THAT LOVE MUST BE REBORN, RE-BORN.


This song was originally written to celebrate the fiftieth birthday of the Iona Community. Based on Leviticus 25 vv. 8–17 (which tells of God's Jubilee), it demonstrates how our faith continually demands that justice and peace become realities for all God's people.

# CHANTS AND RESPONSES

Beneath each text are suggestions for use.

## FOR YOURS IS THE KINGDOM

FOR YOURS IS THE KINGDOM, THE POWER AND THE GLORY
FOR EVER AND EVER, AMEN.
FOR YOURS IS THE KINGDOM, THE POWER AND THE GLORY
FOR EVER AND EVER, AMEN.

This may be used as a sung ascription at the end of the Lord's Prayer, or as a closing chant at the end of worship.

On one occasion we used this, while participants in a service; we came to the crossing (it was a cathedral!) and there laid squares of paper, which each person had been given, in the shape of a cross. The squares were coloured purple, red and gold, symbolising kingdom, power and glory.

## HE BECAME POOR

HE BECAME POOR THAT WE MAY BE RICH,
LOVING THE WORLD AND LEAVING HIS THRONE;
KING OF ALL KINGS AND LORD OF ALL LORDS,
FLESH OF OUR FLESH AND BONE OF OUR BONE.

As a gathering chant, this is particularly useful during Advent and the Christmas season. But it can be used at other times of the year either to intersperse readings from the Life of Christ or as a devotional song when people are reflecting on their vocation or commitment.

## BE STILL

BE STILL AND KNOW THAT I AM GOD.
BE STILL AND KNOW THAT I AM GOD.

A piano or guitar accompaniment is required for best effect when this simple song is used. Voices are divided into two, singing the same tune but starting a bar after each other. It can be used whenever there is a desire to move people from a lively time of worship into a more meditative period or into silence.

## MISERERE NOBIS

MISERERE NOBIS,
MISERERE NOBIS, DOMINE.

(Have mercy on us, O Lord)

When in a prayer of confession, there are short sentences which remind people of where they have failed in their discipleship, this short phrase may be sung as a response.

## O BROTHER JESUS

O BROTHER JESUS, WHERE HAVE WE LEFT YOU,
SAVIOUR AND LOVER OF ALL?

As with *Miserere Nobis*, this phrase is a sung response in a prayer of confession. As a meditation it may be possible to lift from the Bible a sequence of places where Jesus was active and where he is still active:

e.g.   You sat among the forgotten folk, and still you sit among them.

You knelt beside those who were scandalised, and still you kneel beside them.

After each location, the chant could be sung to remind people of the places in which Christ is forgotten and waits to be recognised.

## AARONIC BLESSING

THE LORD BLESS YOU AND KEEP YOU;
THE LORD MAKE HIS FACE TO SHINE UPON YOU
AND BE GRACIOUS UNTO YOU;
THE LORD LIFT UP HIS COUNTENANCE UPON YOU
AND GIVE YOU PEACE.

This blessing may be used at baptisms, confirmations, ordinations, weddings or wherever a stage in the life of God's people invokes the singing of words such as these.

# THE NINIAN SETTING

This setting of chants and responses for Holy Communion is named after the Celtic saint who headed a community at Whithorn, in South West Scotland, in the 5th century.

## KYRIE

KYRIE ELEISON.
CHRISTE ELEISON,
KYRIE ELEISON.

>Lord, have mercy. Christ have mercy, Lord have mercy.

## SANCTUS

SANCTUS, SANCTUS, SANCTUS DOMINUS,
PLENI SUNT COELI ET TERRA GLORIA TUA.

>Holy, holy, holy Lord,
>Heaven and earth are full of your glory.

## BENEDICTUS

BENEDICTUS QUI VENIT IN NOMINE DOMINI.
HOSANNA IN EXCELSIS.

>Blessed is he who comes in the name of the Lord.
>Hosanna in the highest.

## AGNUS DEI

AGNUS DEI QUI TOLLIS PECCATA MUNDI,
MISERERE NOBIS.
DONA NOBIS PACEM.

>O Lamb of God, you take away the sin of the world;
>Have mercy on us.
>Grant us your peace.

# FOR YOURS IS THE KINGDOM

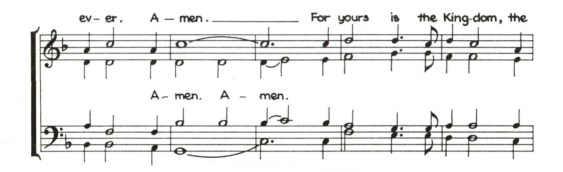

music © 1989 The Iona Community

# HE BECAME POOR

# BE STILL

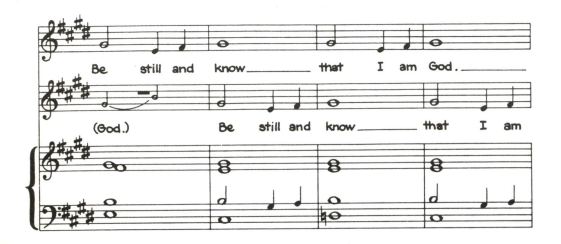

# MISERERE NOBIS

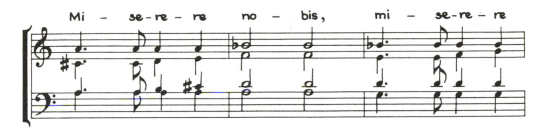

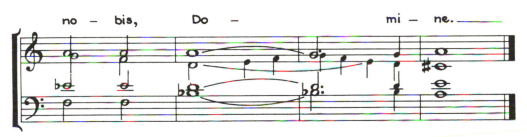

music © 1989 The Iona Community

# O BROTHER JESUS

words and music © 1989 The Iona Community

# AARONIC BLESSING

The Lord bless you and keep you. The Lord make his face to shine up-

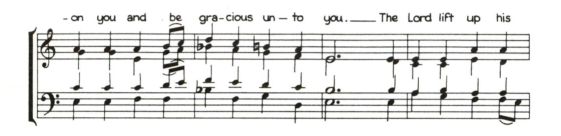

-on you and be gra-cious un—to you. The Lord lift up his

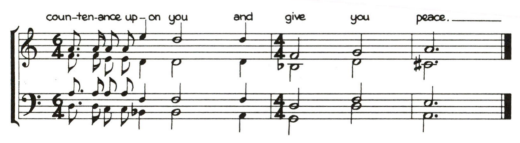

coun-ten-ance up—on you and give you peace.

music © 1989 The Iona Community

## KYRIE

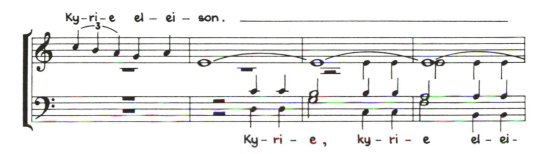

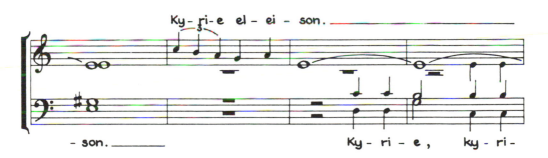

# SANCTUS

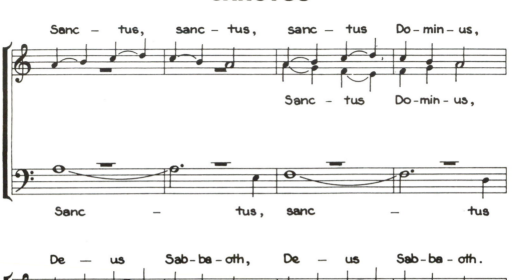

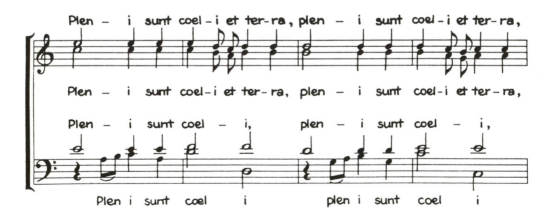

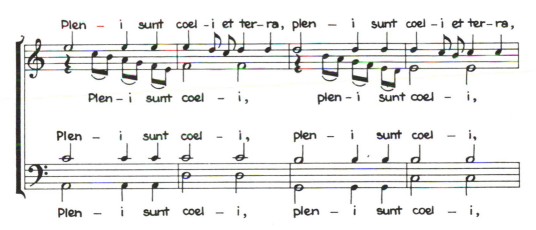

# BENEDICTUS

# AGNUS DEI

(v.1,2&3)Ag – nus     de – i qui tol – is pec-ca – ta, pec-ca – ta mun – di,

mis – er-er- e     no – bis,     mis – er-er- e     no – bis,
(v.3) do – na no-bis pa – cem,     do – na no-bis pa – cem,

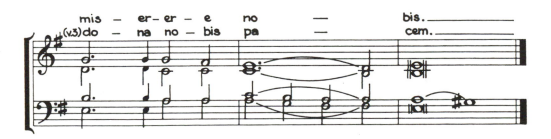

mis – er-er- e     no ——— bis. _____
(v.3)do – na no – bis pa ——— cem. _____

# LOVE FROM BELOW
## Wild Goose Songs — Volume 3
### Alphabetical Index of First Lines

14   A little child in a bed of night
141   Agnus dei qui tollis peccata
104   Among us and before us, Lord, you stand
72   As if you were not there
134   Be still and know that I am God
106   Before I take the body of my Lord
140   Benedictus qui venit
56   Blessed, blessed are you poor
110   Bread is blessed and broken
66   Christ's is the world in which we move
42   Come, Holy Ghost, soon we should be sleeping
94   Come, host of heaven's high dwelling place
102   Come, Lord, be our guest
16   Conceiver of both heaven and earth
126   Every fiftieth year set the captives free
120   For all the saints who've shown your love
132   For yours is the kingdom
122   From Erin's shores Columba came
64   From heaven's attendant host you came
22   God beyond glory, gracious and holy
34   God give us peace that lasts
18   God, in the planning and purpose of life
48   God it was who said to Abraham
84   God the Creator, you in love made me
133   He became poor that we may be rich
62   He knew the greatness of the small
32   Hear me, Lord, and draw near
100   How can we live as Christians here
52   I am the Vine and you the branches
60   I sit outside the rich world's gate
92   Jesus calls us here to meet him
41   Jesus Christ, Lord of all
116   Jesus is risen from the grave
30   Just as a lost and thirsty deer
137   Kyrie eleison
76   Listen, Lord, listen, Lord
24   Lord and lover of creation
135   Miserere nobis
38   Nears the ending of the day
135   O Brother Jesus, where have we left you
36   O Christ, you wept when grief was raw
114   O look and learn that all you earn
112   O taste and see how gracious the Lord is

| 98 | Praise the Lord, the ground of goodness |
| 138 | Sanctus, sanctus, sanctus Dominus |
| 118 | Shout for joy! The Lord has let us feast |
| 96 | Sing and be glad for this is God's house |
| 70 | Sing praise to God on mountain tops |
| 86 | Take this moment, sign and space |
| 20 | That human life might richer be |
| 124 | The God of all eternity |
| 136 | The Lord bless you and keep you |
| 50 | Though one with God, yet not by might |
| 78 | Time, if only I had time |
| 12 | Today I awake and God is before me |
| 26 | Unsure, when what was bright turns dark |
| 68 | We cannot measure how you heal |
| 108 | We who live by sound and symbol |
| 82 | We will lay our burden down |
| 74 | We will not take what is not ours |

## COPYRIGHT

## OTHER PUBLICATIONS

The Iona Community has an increasing range of worship and resource materials, tapes etc., which may be purchased on a retail basis or wholesale. For a catalogue and further details, apply to Wild Goose Resources Group at the above address.

## Wild Goose Publications
# CURRENT PUBLICATIONS OF THE IONA COMMUNITY

| | | |
|---|---|---|
| THE WHOLE EARTH SHALL CRY GLORY Iona prayers by Rev. George F. MacLeod | | ISBN 0 947988 00 9 |
| RE-INVENTING THEOLOGY | Fraser | ISBN 0 947988 29 7 |
| LIVING A COUNTERSIGN – From Iona To Basic Christian Communities | Fraser | ISBN 0 947988 39 4 |
| ROGER – An Extraordinary Peace Campaigner | Steven | ISBN 0 947988 38 6 |
| A WAY TO GOD – A Biography of George More | More ed Ferguson | ISBN 0 947988 45 9 |
| REBUILDING THE COMMON LIFE | Iona Community | ISBN 0 947988 25 4 |
| COLUMBA | Bunting | ISBN 0 947988 11 4 |
| FALLEN TO MEDIOCRITY | Cramb | ISBN 0 947988 46 7 |
| THE IONA COMMUNITY WORSHIP BOOK    Iona Community | | ISBN 0 947988 50 5 |
| HEAVEN SHALL NOT WAIT (Wild Goose Songs Volume 1) | Bell & Maule | ISBN 0 947988 23 8 |
| HEAVEN SHALL NOT WAIT – Cassette | Wild Goose Worship Group | No. IC/WGP/011 |
| ENEMY OF APATHY (Wild Goose Songs Volume 2) | Bell & Maule | ISBN 0 947988 27 0 |
| LOVE FROM BELOW (Wild Goose Songs Volume 3) | Bell & Maule | ISBN 0 947988 34 3 |
| LOVE FROM BELOW – Cassette | Wild Goose Worship Group | No. IC/WGP/008 |
| INNKEEPERS AND LIGHT SLEEPERS (Seventeen new songs for Christmas) | Bell | ISBN 0 947988 47 5 |
| INNKEEPERS AND LIGHT SLEEPERS – Cassette | Wild Goose Worship Group | No. IC/WGP/012 |
| MANY AND GREAT (World Church Songs Volume 1) | Bell & Maule | ISBN 0 947988 40 8 |
| MANY AND GREAT – Cassette | Wild Goose Worship Group | No. IC/WGP/009 |
| SENT BY THE LORD (World Church Songs Volume 2) | Bell & Maule | ISBN 0 947988 44 0 |
| SENT BY THE LORD – Cassette | Wild Goose Worship Group | No. IC/WGP/010 |
| A TOUCHING PLACE – Cassette | Wild Goose Worship Group | No. IC/WGP/004 |
| CLOTH FOR THE CRADLE – Cassette | Wild Goose Worship Group | No. IC/WGP/007 |
| FOLLY AND LOVE – Cassette | Iona Abbey | No. IC/WGP/005 |
| FREEDOM IS COMING – Cassette | Fjedur | No. IC/WGP/006 |
| FREEDOM IS COMING | Utryck | ISBN 91 86788 15 7 |
| PRAISING A MYSTERY | Wren | ISBN 0 947988 36 X |
| BRING MANY NAMES | Wren | ISBN 0 947988 37 8 |
| WILD GOOSE PRINTS No. 1 | Bell & Maule | ISBN 0 947988 06 8 |
| WILD GOOSE PRINTS No. 2 | Bell & Maule | ISBN 0 947988 10 6 |
| WILD GOOSE PRINTS No. 3 | Bell & Maule | ISBN 0 947988 24 6 |
| WILD GOOSE PRINTS No. 4 | Bell & Maule | ISBN 0 947988 35 1 |
| WILD GOOSE PRINTS No. 5 | Bell & Maule | ISBN 0 947988 41 6 |
| WILD GOOSE PRINTS No. 6 | Bell & Maule | ISBN 0 947988 42 4 |
| EH...JESUS...YES, PETER...? Book 1 | Bell & Maule | ISBN 0 947988 20 3 |
| EH...JESUS...YES, PETER...? Book 2 | Bell & Maule | ISBN 0 947988 31 9 |
| EH...JESUS...YES, PETER...? Book 3 | Bell & Maule | ISBN 0 947988 43 2 |
| CORACLE Magazine (current issue) | | Series 3 |

# Wild Goose Publications